Hypnosis Techniques

*Top Hypnosis Techniques for Mind Control
and Persuasion.
Learn How to Manipulate Others and
Get Them to Do What You Want
(2022 Guide for Beginners)*

Alan Wikinson

CONTENT LIST

INTRODUCTION

Most people's perceptions of hypnosis are shaped by what they see in movies. So, when you hear the word, you could imagine a goateed man wearing a large hat, clutching a staff in one hand and flashing a pocket watch in the other. He swings it back and forth until his subject is in a zombie-like state, devoid of free will and under the evil spell of the goateed hypnotist.

The unlucky hypnotised victim will subsequently be obliged to execute the hypnotist's command without question, but as you know, real life isn't like in the movies. Actual hypnosis bears little or no relation to how it is portrayed in films, television shows, and comic books. There's a reason they're called works of fiction.

One of the most mystifying and understandably misunderstood concepts is hypnosis. It has been a source of contention for over 200 years. Many people are unaware that individuals have been entering trances for thousands of years.

This hypnotic trance is induced in many forms of meditation, which are practised by many civilisations. Until the late 1700s, no one seemed to notice it.

Franz Mesner, an Austrian physician who is now regarded as the father of contemporary hypnotism, developed the first scientific notion of hypnotism. His idea of hypnotism, however, was not accepted at the time.

Mesmer defined hypnosis as a mystical power sent from the hypnotist to the subject. This occurrence was dubbed "animal magnetism" by him. The mere suggestion of magic in his definition threw critics off. However, his notion of power derived from a hypnotist and administered to a subject persisted with him for a long time.

Hypnosis is derived from the Greek word Hypnos, which means "sleep." However, hypnosis is not a sleep-like state. In truth, an individual is cognizant while under hypnosis. He has increased focus and concentration. His imagination is also heightened. Every other stimulus in his environment is muffled. He may focus his attention on a specific thought or memory by limiting peripheral awareness, and his capacity to respond to recommendations is increased.

With that said, real-life hypnosis contrasts the popular yet mistaken image of hypnosis in movies. To begin with, a person who is hypnotised is not in a semi-sleep condition. He is awake, aware, and hyper-conscious, which leads us to the second point of conflict. A person in a hypnotic trance does not lose their free will. He does not become a hypnotist's slave.

Most individuals are unaware that they routinely experience this condition of human awareness. Every day, people subject themselves to self-hypnosis. Have you ever become engrossed in a genuinely fantastic book? Have you ever become so involved in your current activity that you lose track of time or your surroundings? People are not precisely sleeping during all of these activities. They are constantly on guard. However, their focus is so intense that practically every other concept has been ruled out.

A person is relaxed while he is in a trance condition. The mind is less restrained. The individual is less cognizant of his actions. You may have noticed that going to the cinema allows you to forget about your issues at work or at home temporarily. When individuals watch a movie, they tend to feel joyful once a pleasant scene or a happy ending is shown.

When the monster in a horror film appears out of nowhere, their hearts race; this is a type of hypnosis in and of itself.

How Does Hypnotism Work?

There are other theories based on hypnosis, but this is the most widely accepted. Hypnosis is considered a direct method of reaching someone's subconscious mind.

Our subconscious mind collaborates with our conscious mind. While the latter makes us aware of information, the former operates in the background, providing us with memory access. Our conscious mind causes us to think critically and realistically, whereas our subconscious mind causes us to think more freely with imagination and impulse.

When we're trying to solve a problem, for example, we examine the facts and brainstorm options deliberately, but the "aha" moments usually come to us intuitively. It's like being stuck on a problem and then suddenly thinking of a solution. The thought is generated by our subconscious.

The subconscious is also in charge of the tasks we do instinctively, such as breathing. It is also the one that analyses and interprets the physical information that our bodies send us. In other words, while our conscious mind is in the forefront, it is our subconscious mind that is at work behind the scenes.

Hypnosis is the key to directly accessing the subconscious without being filtered by the conscious consciousness.

Focusing and deep relaxation techniques, according to doctors, are helpful in making us feel peaceful. They also act to subdue our consciousness, causing it to take a back seat while the subconscious takes centre stage. This is why, while under hypnosis, a person retains full awareness but is very suggestible.

Keep in mind that the unconscious mind wants to be free, but the conscious mind wants to be filtered. The hypnotist communicates directly with the subject's subconscious. The more inventive and impulsive subconscious mind takes over with the conscious mind in the back seat. The individual's responses to recommendations and compulsions are more automatic. Because the subconscious governs the body's senses—visual, tactile, auditory, and so on—as well as the emotions, the hypnotist can trigger the subconscious.

Subject's emotions Furthermore, a person's memory is kept in the subconscious. As a result, while under hypnosis, the individual can recall experiences from the past that have been buried for a long time. Psychiatrists can assist a client in resolving current concerns by digging out these memories. Furthermore, false memories might be created because the mind is in a suggestible condition during hypnosis. As a result, psychiatrists must exercise extreme caution while employing hypnosis to retrieve a patient's recollection of the past.

CHAPTER 1:

WHAT IS HYPNOSIS, AND WHY IS IT USED?

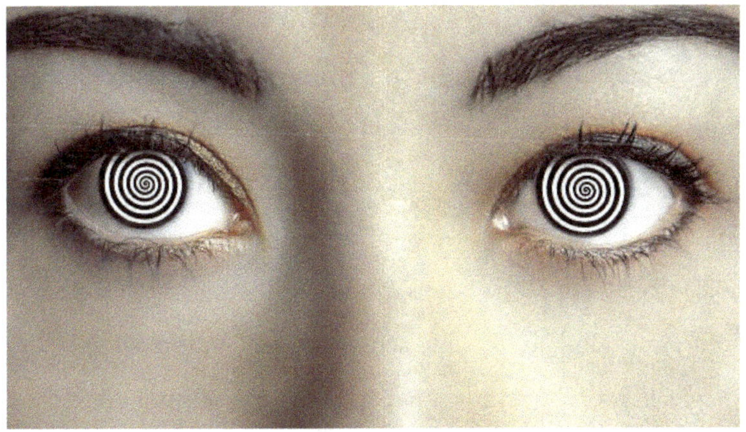

A Basic Overview of Hypnosis, Its History, and Its Benefits

Before we go into the practical application of hypnosis, with step-by-step directions and the actual "how-to," let's lay the groundwork. This understanding will enable you to use the strategies described in this book strategically, wisely, and confidently.

From the ancient Greek word "Hypnos" and the suffix "is," the term "hypnosis" literally means "putting to sleep." It should be noted, however, that hypnosis is not a type of sleep. It is a state of altered relaxation of the mind and body in which the person's attention is intensely concentrated, and they are incredibly receptive to suggestions.

In essence, hypnosis is the process of entering a form of trance, which can be self-produced or caused by another else. It has a long history dating back thousands of years. Meditation, for example, is a form of an altered, trance-like condition, and the sensation of being hypnotised is sometimes linked to the sense of meditation. Being in a trance is more common than you might believe; zoning out on the bus or train is just one example! With a more goal-oriented approach, people have been researching and experiencing altered experiences like this in religious and non-religious contexts all over the world for millennia. Much of it is chronicled in Eastern philosophical and religious texts, such as Hinduism and Buddhism.

The ancient Oracle of Delphi was claimed to have given prophecies while in a trance-like state, while certain Christian saints were said to have talked in ecstasies, and Norse warriors were said to have employed heightened states in combat.

All of this points to the fact that we can change our own experiences in the name of achieving our goals. This natural power is harnessed and shaped into a tool for self-improvement by hypnosis.

The first medically documented hypnotic trance was performed in 1027 by a doctor named Avicenna. However, due to the writings credited to Franz Mesmer, hypnotism became more well known in the medical field much later in the late 18th century.

Mesmer, whose name appears in the word "mesmerise," performed what he named "mesmerism."

He proposed that fluid or force in the universe known as "animal magnetism" impacted us. This energy has the potential to affect our minds, bodies, and spirits and can be manipulated in order to promote healing. He began to test this on patients, and the results appeared to be positive. People naturally worried about what he was doing and whether it was real. What was this animal magnetism he mentioned? In 1784, he was investigated by a board, and it was determined that his work produced valid results. The link to a magical fluid, however, proved erroneous.

The committee decided that Mesmer's actions had a placebo-like effect, and patients benefited from the power of belief and imagination.

Scientist James Braid (1795 – 1860) was interested in the events and results observed in Mesmer's patients, and he attempted to explain them further using the scientific method and physical laws. He demonstrated that captivated or induced trance patients exhibited changes such as concentrated attention and sensitivity to suggestions. This paved the path for more research into the relationship between mind and body, which is still ongoing to this day.

Michel Chevreul's (1786-1889) classic experiment reveals suggestibility and the power of the mind-body link in a way that you may easily replicate at home right now. It is popularly known as a pendulum experiment, which is both entertaining and enlightening. This experiment is fascinating because it demonstrates how the mind and body interact in an essential and elegant manner. Here's how it works:

Make a circle out of a piece of paper. Cut that circle into four quadrants, beginning at the top. Moving clockwise, label each point of the cross: A, B, C, and D.

Make a pendulum now. Tie a weight to the bottom of a piece of string. A ring is sufficient.

Prepare to sit comfortably at a table. Place the paper on the table and your elbow on top of it, holding the pendulum between your thumb and forefinger at the centre of the cross. Hold your elbow steady, relax your arm, but keep it still.

Concentrate your attention on the pendulum now. Keep it fixed in place and picture the pendulum swinging from side to side. Visualise it in your mind's eye. Consider how you feel when you visualise the pendulum swinging. Make this image as vivid as you can.

What did you observe? The pendulum begins to sway. Now you may start messing around with it. Can you get it to swing faster? Which way do you want to go? What's the point of going around in circles? Isn't it quite potent? It makes you consider all of your thoughts and how they affect your body, life, current circumstances, and the globe. The most astounding aspect of this is that we actually have much control!

Going back in time, after it was discovered that there is a link between the mind and the body, modern psychologists adapted, practised, and researched the application of hypnosis from a scientific position to aid their patients.

Among these are Pierre Janet and Sigmund Freud. The latter was particularly interested in helping his patients connect with and release repressed memories, which is something that highly qualified and licenced clinical psychologists still utilise hypnosis for today, but which we will not discuss in this book.

Milton Erickson was a hypnosis proponent who pioneered the use of metaphor, confusion, and indirect suggestion techniques. He was one-of-a-kind and highly effective in his methods. Later in the novel, you'll learn more about him.

Today, hypnotherapy is widely employed to treat a wide range of medical issues. These include, among other things, anxiety, stress, and addictions such as smoking or gambling, insomnia, PTSD, eating disorders, weight loss, controlling pain, and assisting with relaxing.

It may also be used in goal planning and other self-help tactics to overcome limiting beliefs and concerns, allowing a person to become more successful in their job, relationships, and sports or other fields.

So, now that we've covered the basics of hypnosis, what exactly is it? What distinguishes hypnosis? Here are the fundamentals

First, consider suggestibility. Hypnosis is a hyper-suggestible state. According to studies, people's suggestibility varies, with a small percentage being very highly suggestible, a small number being less suggestible, and the bulk falling somewhere in the middle. Studies also demonstrate that no matter where you are on the spectrum, hypnosis and the power of suggestion can help you.

Second, there is separation. This is the act of putting one's judgement or critical thinking aside. It's a routine process that everyone goes through regularly. This includes imagining, "zoning out," and retreating somehow. These are natural ways for us to recharge or process information. Some persons are predisposed to dissociation more than others.

The third characteristic is absorption, which is a form of focus. This is what it's like to be entirely immersed in something. Have you ever read a book and felt as if the rest of the world had vanished and you were wholly engaged in the storey? Perhaps you experienced this while watching a movie or a TV show. That's how I feel.

Relaxation is the fourth step. Relaxation of the mind and body makes it easier to be hypnotised.

Some recent views concerning why and how hypnosis works include that of Robert Baker, a psychologist who argues that when we are hypnotised, we are submitting to and following a set of formal and social standards. In other words, when certain conditions are met, participants take on the role of being hypnotised. The TEAM hypothesis expands on this concept in an efficient way, claiming that hypnosis comprises a range of states such as relaxation, expectancy, motivation, and anticipation. TEAM is an acronym that stands for Trust, Expectation, Attitude, and Motivation.

Scientific study shows that hypnosis is an effective tool. Although we do not fully understand how it works, it is advantageous to those who want to grow, change, or improve their life in some way.

You'll be able to understand what you're doing in your practice and what may or may not be happening in your subjects when you deal with them now that you know where it came from and some of the science behind it.

So, let's get started and figure out how it's done!

CHAPTER 2:

TECHNIQUES OF HYPNOSIS

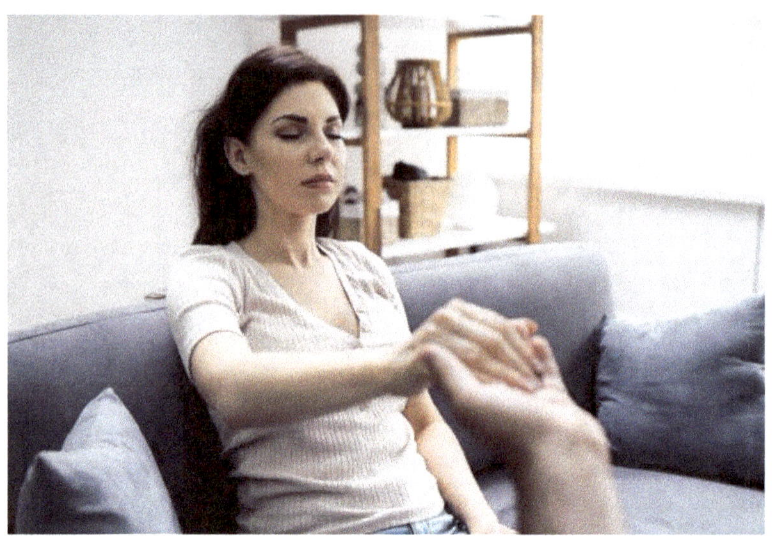

Once you have mastered the long hypnosis process, you may begin to use another vital form of hypnosis to your benefit, quick hypnosis. These tactics play with the fundamentals of the mind and what can happen to anyone daily. Have you ever looked out the window and just watched the rainfall? What about listening to music that soothes and relaxes you? Perhaps you're watching a beloved movie or television show, and you find yourself tuning out.

When this happens, you may not even realise since you are comfortable, relaxed, and entirely absorbed in what you are doing.

It occurs daily and has three distinguishing features.

1. Increased concentration and focus.

2. Increased bodily relaxation.

3. Improved access to the subconscious mind

Hypnosis merely leverages this natural condition of affairs to place your patient into that frame of mind swiftly.

The Handshake Method

This strategy necessitates some level of trust between you and the subject. As you extend out your hand to shake theirs and then draw them sharply in towards yourself, say the word sleep forcefully but quietly. If you don't establish a little trust between you, this could backfire and make the topic tense when you pull them close. How did this method work so well? It works by inducing hypnosis through two distinct processes: throwing the individual off balance so the brain does not have time to compute a response and making a solid recommendation of sleep that appears to the brain to be a desirable choice.

People are a lot more suggestive than they realise, which is how this basic but effective immediate strategy works.

Method of Falling Backwards

This type of rapid hypnosis works by throwing someone off balance and offering them a suggestion to follow. However, the subject will lean slightly backwards instead of drawing them forward towards you. This procedure can put your issue under in less than a minute by following simple steps:

Step 1:

Have your subjects stand with their feet together and their arms at their sides. As they progress, explain what you will be doing with them step by step so that they understand what is coming next. You will also inform them that this would put their relaxation reflexes to the test.

Step 2:

Take an action back and place both hands on your subject's shoulders. Stand close enough to control them as they descend, but not so close that they land on you. Control the fall, but don't put too much weight on it.

Put one foot in front of the other, and you'll be able to maintain the proper balance to support their weight as they fall back. Inform the individual that this is only a practice run.

Step 3:

Ask your subject to relax and explain that you will pull them back a few inches but will not let them fall. Make it clear that you will not allow them to fall, and instruct them to remain relaxed and bend their bodies just at the ankles, not the waist, knees, or anywhere else.

Step 4:

Keeping your hands on the subject's shoulders, ask them to close their eyes and pull their gaze back a few inches. A two or three-inch gap is sufficient. Remember not to jar or force them, but instead to let them gradually tip backwards and then rock forward again. Keep your hands firmly on their shoulders and bring the client back up to their feet, making sure they have regained their equilibrium.

Step 5:

If your subject appears to be at ease, proceed to the next step. If not, reassure the issue that they have done well and repeat the previous stage to ensure the subject understands what to expect. Certain apprehensive subjects may require multiple attempts before they are entirely comfortable.

Step 6:

After they have fallen back, seat them down and utilise a short and brief deepening procedure to ensure they are deeply hypnotised. This is typically accomplished by repeating phrases such as "go deeper and deeper into hypnosis, relax" as needed to ensure that your client is deeply immersed in hypnosis.

The Eye Exam

You want to use this simple approach to affirm for both you and the subject that a state of hypnosis has been achieved with an instant technique. With your issue comfortably seated, go through the following steps:

1st step:

"You have the sensation that your eyes are quite heavy and completely relaxed. Every muscle in their vicinity is now relaxed. This causes your eyelids to be quite heavy."

Step two:

"I will ask you to open your eyes on the count of three, not before. You won't be able to answer when I ask. Your eyelids are excessively heavy since you are entirely relaxed. You won't be able to open your eyes because your eyelids are so heavy, and you'll be so comfortable that you won't even attempt."

Step three:

"Your eyelids are shut. Heavy. They are sealed up and cannot be opened."

4th step:

"The first. Your eyes are closed, and your eyelids are drooping. You can't open them, no matter how hard you try. You just cannot open them because they are far too hefty."

5th step:

"Two. You are unable to open your eyes."

Sixth step:

"Three, your eyes are firmly shut. Try to open them. You know you can't open them, right? Your eyelids are droopy. Stop attempting; simply relax your eyes again; no more attempting to open them. As your eyes should be, so should your body. Relax."

When doing this procedure, be sure that you do not allow the victim to open their eyes for more than a second or two. If you give them too much time, they will finally be able to force their eyes open, and they will emerge out of hypnosis. If they can open their eyes without any effort, they have not been sedated, and you must begin again. If this happens and they open their eyes, simply tell them it's okay and that their eyes weren't relaxed enough, so you'll start over, remembering to maintain a cheerful attitude.

Relaxation Method

During an initial encounter, therapists would typically ask you to make yourself at ease and comfortable. They might even provide you with a comfortable couch to sleep on. Why? Is it just politeness on their part? The truth is that it is much more than that. Relaxation is a systematic approach used by therapists to induce hypnosis. When you are relaxed, you are more likely to enter a trance, and your mind is more open to accepting suggestions. Some of the most common strategies for promoting relaxation are as follows:

- Make yourself at ease.
- Lie down.
- Begin counting down in your head.
- Keep your breathing under control.
- Tense and then relax your muscles.
- Speak in a gentle, calm tone.

Handshake Method

Milton Erickson, the creator of hypnosis, became famous for inducing a hypnotic trance with a handshake. A handshake is a typical greeting, but it can be more than just a gesture in hypnosis. Hypnotists do not simply shake hands; they disrupt the subject's consciousness by grasping his wrist or dragging him forward to disturb the balance. Because the subject's mind's regular pattern was disrupted, the client's subconscious mind will suddenly be open to suggestions.

Cues from the Eyes Technique

The brain is divided into two parts: the conscious and creative side (on the right) and the practical and subconscious half (on the left) (left). When we're talking to someone, we're looking for feedback to see how they feel or react to what we're saying. Take note of your subject's eyes. Are they orienting themselves to the right? Is it possible that they're staring to the left? Remember that if they are looking to the right, it indicates that they are aware of the current circumstance, and if they are looking to the left, it suggests that they are in subconscious thought

Technique for Visualization

You can employ visualisation to produce a hypnotic trance and suggestions for your subject. For example, ask your person to imagine a room that they are pretty familiar with. Instruct them to envision every feature in the room, including the windows, the fragrance, the lighting, the colour of the walls, and the floor's texture. Then, ask them to imagine a room they've never seen before, such as your workplace. They open their minds to suggestions while attempting to remember the exact details of the room they are less familiar with.

Technique for Arm Levitation

You can accomplish this by having your patient close their eyes. Then, ask them to identify any differences in their arms. They may claim that their arms are heavy or light. Subconsciously, they will enter a trance and either lift their arms or convince their minds that they have raised their arms. In any case, the induction was a success.

The technique of Sudden Shock/Falling Backwards

Like the handshake technique, a subject in shock can enter a trance. You may have heard the phrase "trust falls." The sensation of falling backwards can startle the body. As a result, it prepares the mind to accept suggestions. Of course, you must catch your subject and avoid dropping them.

The technique of Hypnotic Triggering

There are various types of hypnotic stimuli. A trigger is a device that allows the subconscious to recall a desired mood or action that was recommended while under hypnosis. Following are some examples:

- Clap
- The sound of the ball
- Opening one's eyes
- Standing or sitting
- Snaping fingers

Technique of Touch

In this procedure, the hypnotist or psychiatrist will induce a state of relaxation in the subject. The hypnotist will next lightly tap the subject's hands with their own with light pressure. Then, with a pen immediately in front of the issue, students will follow it with their eyes while mentally envisioning an ideal location. During each session, this procedure must be repeated numerous times. Every session I have with this technique leaves me relaxed and feeling a lot better.

CHAPTER 3:

THE UGLY SIDE OF HYPNOSIS

The United States CIA (Central Intelligence Agency) attempted to develop the perfect killing machine in the 1950s and 1960s. A programme known as "Project MKUltra" was launched, and "MKUltra" was divided into a slew of subprograms administered by the CIA, FBI, and the US military, with names like "Operation Paperclip" and "Project Monarch." This is not a conspiracy theory in the least. The US government has admitted to it, and many reclassified records reveal that this heinous operation did exist. Not only were American people and heroic warriors drugged and brainwashed without their knowledge, but they were also forced to inhumane life-threatening situations.

One of the largest scandals to emerge from this operation was hypnotising and then administering LSD to an American army scientist. The man's name was Frank Olson, and without his knowledge or agreement, the CIA and other government agencies hypnotised, brainwashed, and administered enormous dosages of the potent hallucinogenic drug LSD to him, also known as LSD Under false pretences, CIA operatives and doctors lured Frank Olson to a hotel room and spiked his drink with LSD in the name of science. As you can expect, Mr Olson became irritated and confused by what was going on, and he ended up smashing through a plate glass window on the 23rd level in utter hysteria and falling to his untimely and tragic death.

The government investigated and determined that they had done nothing wrong, and Mr Olson's death was ruled a tragic suicide. Of course, the family knew that couldn't be true, so they pressed the authorities further, and it was reluctantly categorised as a "misadventure."

The surviving family and a large number of other individuals believe it was a murder, especially after the case's records were reclassified and the illicit drug tests were uncovered. Mr Olson, however, was not the only victim of Project MKUltra.

Another example from that project involves a man who was repeatedly hypnotised and given LSD to consume for 145 days in a row. Another unsettling paper discloses a study in which two women were hypnotised using a powerful new technique. One lady was placed in a deep hypnotic slumber, and the second woman was told to wake her up. If the other woman did not wake up, she was told to pull the trigger on a gun she had been given and shoot the woman in the head. Fortunately, the gun wasn't loaded since that's precisely what she did. Another case included a woman who was hypnotised and told to wait by phone. Then she received a phone call, and a secret code phrase was whispered into her ear. Following this prompting, the woman entered a profound trance and felt obliged to carry a bag containing a bogus bomb and place it beneath a bridge. It has even been claimed that the CIA has utilised mind control and hypnosis to split a person's personality into different sections where one character is unaware of what the other is doing in order to carry out hidden clandestine missions. It's the ideal scenario if they're divided into separate people with distinct personalities, just like

"The Manchurian Candidate, a film about the government's use of mind control. A very terrible person or nation may utilise this to put a person close enough to assassinate a President or even the Pope. Brainwashing someone with hypnosis is a heinous crime in and of itself, but this is not the first time that hypnotism and mesmerism have been employed for wicked purposes. Consider a specific man in Germany during WWII who used his great hypnotic technique to incite a country to war and persuade the German people that burning people in large steel ovens was friendly.

Hitler did not begin his career as a superb orator. He practised his body movements in front of a full-length mirror to ensure they were perfect. He schooled himself to speak in a forceful, booming voice that would stimulate the minds of ordinary Germans. His eyes were so magnificent and piercing that even if you couldn't comprehend what he was saying, you could sense his immense animal magnetism that captivated everyone. Everything had to be just right in order to enchant the adoring crowds.

Hitler would order massive rituals in which hundreds of thousands of men, women, and children waved small flags and soldiers marched in perfect synchrony while hundreds of runners carrying torches jogged through the area. It was quite a show, and he had them eating right out of his hands. They didn't wake up from their hypnotic trance and realise him for what he indeed was until it was too late.

What about the modern world? Indeed, in this day and age, we are not being mesmerised and brainwashed? Yes, we are... more so than ever before. Thanks to the clever use of hypnotic propaganda, today's government have so much power over us that we don't know whether we're coming or departing. The government instructs significant media outlets on what to print to elicit a reaction favouring them and advancing their agenda. Every major newspaper's front page will feature the same top storey on any given day. People are fascinated by their cellphones, as seen by footage of people falling into open utility holes while staring closely at their video phones. If they aren't engrossed in the activities on their phones, they are usually staring droopily at a computer monitor with their lips open. Facebook has them mesmerized.

The internet is the perfect hypnotic instrument for the government to impose its agenda while keeping people lovely and tranquil. We don't want revolutions, do we? The unfortunate aspect of this government control is that we, the citizens, are complicit in it. However, it is not entirely fair to blame the citizenry for falling prey to the hypnotic trap; after all, we have been hypnotically conditioned to fall into line since we entered preschool. Nowadays, we actually invite a hypnotic gadget into our homes, such as Amazon's Alexa machine, so that the government may listen in on and record our private chats.

What needs to be done is for people to be more aware of the hypnotic influence that is being imposed on them. Educate yourself and attempt to be more attentive as you go about your daily activities. Simply give up the entrancing screen of the internet for a week. Read alternative papers (as long as they're reputable), be a decent citizen, and vote. It is feasible to get rid of those who are attempting to control us and replace them with congressmen and senators who would abolish the "nanny state" that we now live in. Every day, businesses enchant us. They are pretty skilled at manipulating our brains through the use of our senses. We are titillated by sexy images of bikini-clad supermodels and muscular hunks assuring us that if we only buy the product they are endorsing, we can be like them. When our leaders repeat the same lies over and over, it's a type of hypnosis. "If you tell a falsehood enough times, it becomes the truth," Joseph Goebbels declared while working as Adolph Hitler's publicity minister.

CHAPTER 4:

HYPNOTIC CONNECTION CREATED THROUGH EMOTION

When it comes to influencing, persuading, and connecting with others, elevated emotional states are highly effective. Consider what it would be like to elicit any emotion from a person. Consider the power you would have to persuade them. Do you feel the strength in doing this, as I do? (Notice what I did there?)

You may quickly send a pleasant or negative sentiment to your target and associate that emotion with any location or object you wish.

I know some business owners that use this in an unscrupulous manner. They will elicit a strong unfavourable response in their consumer or prospect and associate that unpleasant emotion with their competition. The same is true for romantic interests. I've seen people manipulate a love interest into feeling a very unpleasant feeling and then connect that emotion to their existing relationship, eliciting a happy emotion and getting their love interest to relate that to them. You can only imagine the moral and ethical ramifications of this. But keep in mind that manipulating others into doing something they don't want to do will come back to bite the manipulator in the buttocks.

Manipulating or coercing someone to do something they don't want to do or buy something they don't want to buy is not the same as persuading them. Persuading is the process of influencing a person's behaviour or decision to make that decision easier. People will frequently buy something on a whim or because they are moved by a particular emotion, even though they do not require or desire the item. When they arrive home, they frequently realise, or at least pause, and think, "Wait, I didn't want or need it." Why did I buy that?

I'm returning it!" Buyer's remorse ensues, and the victim frequently regrets their decision, feels taken advantage of and resents the person they believe took advantage of them.

Remember that emotions are one technique to avoid the critical mind. When a person is in a heightened emotional state, their subconscious mind is more open and sensitive. Whatever happens around or related to that emotional state/time will frequently cause behaviour or response in the target's subconscious mind. You can accomplish this by eliciting a happy or negative emotion and then connecting or relating those emotions to anything to encourage your target to think, feel, or respond in the manner you want them to. Laughter is one of the great ways to break down barriers. When people are smiling and having a good time, their guard is down, and they are easier to persuade since they are not expecting to be sold, swayed, or even learn. One of my favourite compliments is when someone attends one of my classes and says, "Dan, we were laughing and having so much fun that we didn't even realise we were learning!"

Various hypnotic emotion-evoking words can transport a person to a moment when they felt a specific way or create a period when they would feel that way. These emotions that we elicit in others are referred to as "arousal emotions." It's not as bad as it sounds. These are the kinds of emotions that keep your target aware and interested in whatever you're directing their attention to. These feelings should be strong enough to elicit a reaction from individuals, and the emotional buzz phrases will aid in this.

Before invoking emotion using one of the emotional keywords, determine how you want people to feel or how they should feel. What emotions do you want them to have? What should they be feeling? Why should they think that? Now, let's look at some emotive hypnotic buzzwords that can help elicit these feelings.

Emotional Hypnotic Phrases

Imagine, see, envisage, consider, and consider a moment when...

Examples are words and phrases that elicit emotions and feelings in the subconscious mind. Remember that when you evoke emotion, you reach the subconscious mind, allowing your target to visualise themselves feeling good about their decision.

You can use any combination of these terms; in fact, you should! You'll want to vary it because everyone communicates differently. Some people say they can think about something but have trouble picturing it. Others will say they can imagine something but not visualise it, and so forth.

Let's look at some examples of how this can be done.

Let's start with eliciting good sentiments. Let's take a look at an example of asking someone out on a date. "Imagine how much fun we'll have at the baseball game; it'll be just like the time we met each other at Jamie's party and laughed so hard we spilt our drinks!" Do you remember that? I have no idea what we were talking about, do you? So, when should I come to pick you up to take you to the game?"

You want to move them up the emotional ladder to a more favourable condition. We are more likely to agree and say yes when we feel better about something!

This is also useful in a sales environment. Assume you're trying to sell a computer to someone. Before employing any of the emotive keywords, you should first ascertain their motivation for purchasing the laptop. Assume they require a machine that is quicker and has more memory. They're wary of having to wait 5 minutes for the software to launch, and they despise having to carry around an extra hard drive. Knowing this, you could think, "Imagine taking the computer home and being able to use it right away." Say goodbye to all of your previous problems. Consider how much faster you'll be able to do tasks with your new laptop and how much easier it will be to keep everything contained so that you can retire that old external hard drive!"

Positive Emotions as a Foundation

You may already be aware of this, but you can attach a happy or negative emotion just as quickly as you can provoke it.

After eliciting that emotion, have the target imagine themselves feeling that emotion about you, your product, or your service. In the baseball game scenario, we asked the target to recall a time when they felt happy. After accessing that experience, it was linked to the baseball game, and they imagined themselves feeling the same way in the future situation.

You may do the same with negative feelings. Activate them and connect them to something. Without going too political, this is something that a lot of political personalities do. When you see an ad around election time, it begins by creating an adverse reaction by showing some horrific imagery, such as tiny children starving, people dying in a hospital bed, or some other extremely upsetting image. Then it says something like, "This is what will happen if (insert candidate here) is elected."

"People may forget what you say, but they will never forget how you made them feel," Maya Angelou once stated.

So, get out there and arouse some feelings in people. Make them happy, and they'll remember you for it.

The Power of Thrilling Emotions and Love

In my hypnosis practice, I see many patients who are struggling with their confidence. For some, this includes dating confidence. People frequently ask me, "What is the ideal first date?" once we have increased feelings of trust, decreased feelings of worry, and established an unstoppable state of mind.

Many research has been conducted to determine what to do and where to go. Whether you believe it or not, going to the movies is the worst first date you could go on. A reasonable first date should begin with something that raises the level of excitement and releases endorphins. We feel good when we start the flow of endorphins, and the stories of oxytocin and dopamine (the chemicals responsible for love and happiness) also flow. We associate those feelings with the person. If you're going to include supper on your date, it's preferable to do the exciting portion first and then go to dinner afterwards so that you can chat about your pleasant experiences.

CHAPTER 5:

COMMON PROBLEMS THAT CAN BE ADDRESSED IN THE CONNECTION WITH HYPNOSIS

Hypnosis can help with a wide range of challenges that humans face daily. In truth, some outstanding minor issues cannot be resolved by hypnosis. As many individuals have discovered over the last two centuries, hypnosis is an excellent technique to alter, alleviate, reframe, restructure, or recollect events or ailments in your life so that you can go beyond them and establish peace and harmony. I know you're seeking a solution to improve your life; otherwise, you wouldn't have bought this book.

With that in mind, I've included a few ways that hypnosis can help with a variety of common problems that individuals face on a daily basis.

Depression

Depression is a widespread condition that affects many people all over the world. It can be seen in youngsters as young as five years old and adults of various ages. If not treated properly, it can be disabling and even fatal. Many people who suffer from depression miss their family and friends because they are unable to move past the emotional turmoil that occurs when they are in a deep depressive state.

The good news is that hypnosis is an excellent method for coping with these challenges. You can begin to enjoy life more by employing hypnosis. You can live a more confident and joyful life. Despite the fact that depression is caused by a chemical imbalance in the brain, it can be efficiently cured using hypnosis.

Hypnosis can be used to treat depression in a variety of ways. One approach would be to utilise the hypnosis session to reinterpret the events in the person's life that are bringing them the most anguish. This can be employed by reframing the circumstances and transforming the bad into a positive.

Affirmations are one method for changing negative thoughts into good ones. These positive changes can be accomplished through a hypnosis system in which you analyse prior experiences and then adjust how the person sees those events in a more positive perspective, as well as assist them in realising that they are no longer that person and the events that occurred can no longer damage them.

Anxiety

Another mental condition that many people suffer from is anxiety. It is also one that can be altered or reduced by using a relaxation hypnosis technique to help the person go past the fear and into a place where they feel comfortable and secure.

When people experience anxiety, it is usually as a result of a scenario in their lives that has put them in a fight-or-flight mentality. They never learned how to get out of the fight-or-flight mode as a result of this experience, and their bodies now go into this fear-based mode on accidental circumstances that would not usually elicit this type of response. This might lead to a slew of issues in a person's life. Anxiety may be harmful to relationships as well as the mind of the person suffering from it.

They will generate events that elicit the same response and then experience anxiety, even if the stress is illogical. It will prohibit them from leaving their house, causing them to miss out on career chances, meet new people, maintain in touch with loved ones, and, in extreme cases, prevent them from leaving their houses at all, resulting in an even more dangerous illness known as Agoraphobia.

You can begin to lessen anxiety symptoms by adopting a hypnosis method known as relaxation.

- Begin by putting yourself as easy as possible.

- You can lie down or sit in a recliner in a comfortable position. Begin mentally counting down from 1 to 10.

- Slowly inhale through your mouth and exhale through your nose.

- Control your breathing and allow it to be rhythmic, with 4 seconds between each inhalation and exhalation.

- Tense your muscles as you take a deep breath in. Relax your body's muscles as you exhale.

- Speak to yourself in a soothing tone, making positive and affirming phrases that will put you in a more relaxed and tranquil state of mind.

- "I feel comfortable and secure in this place," for example.

Problems with Attitude

Many people have mental health problems. These could be misconceptions that our family has instilled in us since childhood. It can also be behaviours observed in others that have lingered with us and elicited dread, anxiety, or hostile responses in ourselves. Mindset is what defines who we are and what we stand for. It has the power to make or break you. For example, if you are constantly told that you are unworthy of love, you will ruin the potential to experience true love because of the beliefs instilled in you at a young age. This is why it is critical to address these mindset issues and cultivate more positive thinking inside oneself.

You may begin to make more good decisions and improvements in your life once you begin to reframe your mentality. You will be bound to repeat a cycle of disappointments and misery until you cultivate positive thoughts and sentiments. You will see tendencies that only allow you to see the negative in life, and this will create a loop of negativity that will prevent you from seeing the good.

All of this can be helped by hypnosis. You can utilise the identical strategy outlined above for anxiety relief by utilising positive affirmations, but instead of saying, "I am safe and secure in this area," you would use a positive affirmation that would help you reframe your attitude and develop more positive connections inside your mind.

These bridges you will build will assist in reducing emotions of worthlessness and will teach you that you are deserving of beautiful things in your life.

Affirmations can be used in a variety of ways:

- "In life, I am deserving of big things."
- "Everything I do is fantastic."
- "With my words, I create magic."
- "I attract money."
- "I am well-liked by a large number of people."

Quitting Smoking

Many people began smoking at an early age in order to appear cool in front of their friends and peers or to escape from some familial crisis that had turned their world upside down. Smoking is the leading cause of death in the United States and should be addressed like a toxin; nonetheless, many people suffer on a daily basis as a result of their efforts to quit smoking. There are some who can quit smoking without any difficulty. Those, though, are few and far between. There is hypnotherapy for individuals who cannot quickly stop smoking. Hypnotherapy is the use of hypnosis to change the behaviour you want to change.

When you smoke for an extended period of time, you train your body to demand that chemical in order to survive and operate normally. This generates a type of addiction that controls the mind and instructs your mind to crave a cigarette even at inconvenient moments. If you've ever seen an advertisement that promotes quitting smoking, you've seen the power that smoking has over you. If you are a smoker, you may not know how controlling it is until you look at it from a different perspective. People find it challenging to quit smoking because it is so addictive and dominating. This is when hypnosis comes into play.

You will be able to wash the poisons from your body subconsciously and generate a more intense cord-cutting experience from the addiction that is smoking by using a hypnosis technique called smoking cessation. There are various ways or sessions that may be used to quit smoking, and as a qualified hypnotherapist, I recommend finding the one that best meets your needs and then repeating it for weeks until you no longer have the strong desire to smoke. In fact, with the practical application of these techniques, you should be able to entirely break your addiction to smoking after eight weeks of daily hypnotherapy.

Loss of Weight

According to statistics, America is far more overweight than any other country. This is extremely harmful to the health of our country and the health of its people. As a proponent of a healthy weight, I believe that hypnosis is an excellent approach to modifying these statistics and putting the American people in a much healthier mind. You can begin to change your weight and diet by changing your eating habits or the triggers that cause overeating.

Emotional eating is the primary cause of most people's obesity. We are instructed as youngsters to finish our supper dishes even if we are absolutely packed, as well as stuffing our faces with ice cream and pastries when we're down, celebrating, or just watching a movie. This promotes a vicious cycle of overeating. Overeating is defined as eating more than we require. For some of us, this implies junk food, sugary drinks, snacks, fatty foods like pork, beef, and poultry, as well as processed foods with no nutritional value.

You can use behaviour modification to change the way you think about food and arrange your meals. This will be used throughout your hypnosis session to assist cement those changes in your subconscious mind so that you no longer overeat or focus on eating more. It will eliminate your urge to eat for emotional gratification and will teach you healthy food and eating behaviours.

You can make the following changes to your hypnosis session:

- "I no longer require eating to be whole."
- "I eat only what I need to live and nothing more."
- "I no longer let my emotions control how much I eat."
- "I go for a walk when I'm feeling depressed."
- "Food does not provide comfort."

This book is created to assist you in attaining these processes for yourself and offer you a better knowledge of what it may help you achieve. I'll start by testing your suggestibility before moving on to the procedures, inductions, and suggestions found in hypnosis, as well as modification building techniques and how to discriminate between the body language of persons you're hypnotising.

CHAPTER 6:

ESSENTIAL TECHNIQUES AND TOOLS

This section discusses breathing, voice use, and language in order to become a more effective hypnotist.

As a hypnotist, you must have a repertory of scripts and procedures as well as a conceptual grasp of how they interact with the human psyche. Other skills must also be developed to supplement these abilities. Breathing, voice, language use, and remembering are examples of these.

Working with people necessitates a certain amount of energy and concentration on oneself. You will be directing someone through a process; therefore, you should be cognitively, physically, and emotionally prepared ahead of time. When you work with a client, they are putting their faith in your hands in many ways. Thus you must be smart. Learning to breathe in a linked manner can help you stay balanced, aware, and energised. Additionally, if you live, your clients will do the same. You want them to be as comfortable as possible, and breathing will help you lead the way.

Breath

Use this simple technique to reconnect with your breath and refresh your batteries.

Begin by sitting down. Set your feet firmly on the ground. Feel the earth beneath your feet's soles. You have the option of closing your eyes or softening your look. Put your hand where you feel your breath on your body. Feel your diaphragm rise and fall. Allow yourself to exhale and inhale for more extended periods of time. Allow yourself to feel your breath all the way down into your belly. Feel your breath on your chest's sides.

Feel the contraction and expansion of your lungs. Feel the warmth of your breath on your back. Feel your lungs expanding and contracting. Extend your exhalation if you believe your breath is too short. Allow the air to enter you. Keep an eye on your breathing without trying to regulate it. After a few minutes of deep breathing, begin to return to your regular breathing rate. Take a few moments to open your eyes, get up, and get your bearings in the room.

Voice

The voice is our next focus of interest. This is your primary tool for guiding your subject, so make it count. It will take time and attention to develop your voice, but it will pay off if you can use it successfully. The breath is linked to the voice. Your voice is primarily supported by your breath. It enables you to make a sound and aids in the use of resonators (the bony structures that vibrate the sound). Singing scales and having the resonance radiate through your body can help you develop your voice. The following is an excellent approach to release the resonance in your voice:

Stand with your feet slightly apart and in a comfortable position. Bring your knees together. Gently bounce and feel the pressure release from your pelvis. Feel your entire spine spiral up through your torso, balanced on top. On a single note, make an open 'ah' sound. Make this sound as quickly as you can. Feel the vibrations by gently tapping your rib cage. In this resonance, experiment with different notes ranging from high to low. Are you able to feel the slight vibrations in your hands as you move your fingertips to your face and generate higher sounds that reverberate through the interior of your skull? Make a "huh- huh" sound from the centre of your body to gain additional power. Feel your diaphragm contract. Gradually introduce the words: "Hi! And hello!" by employing this strategy. Your voice has now warmed up—experiment with generating louder and softer sounds to learn how to manipulate your voice at will.

Because your client's eyes will be closed, you will primarily use the sound of your voice to instruct them like a hypnotist. At times, you'll want to seem authoritative, at others, warm and soothing, and still, at others, you'll want to emphasise key phrases and concepts.

Take a few moments to consider the voices you've heard throughout your life. Do you have a preference for one over another? Of course, yes. A voice can either soothe you to sleep or grate on your nerves. What does your voice sound like? Many people find this a complicated issue to answer, yet it is necessary to do so. You should record yourself talking to someone while going through the process from beginning to end and then listen to it afterwards. What emotions do you experience when you listen to your own voice? Make a list of ways you could have used it better in different stages of the process. You want to tailor the way you speak to have the desired effect, much like a performance. Pay attention to the sounds you hear; which ones do you find appealing? Adopt their mode of communication if you believe it would be effective.

Here are some principles to follow when it comes to intonation and voice:

- When you say "sleep" in an induction, for example, you want this word to be short and assertive. It's not smooth and mild, but it's also not excessively short, sharp, or aggressive. Try not to startle the client. However, be sure that they hear this unique command.

- A calm, tranquil voice will be more favourable to people letting go and submitting during a relaxing induction. Keep this in mind when you read this section of the script.

- You should use a complex and direct tone of voice to rouse them up.

- Speak simply and loudly, avoiding melody.

Memorization

Learning by heart or memorising is an undervalued skill that will serve you well as a hypnotist and throughout your life. We rely on our phones a lot these days, but knowing a script inside and out will offer you the freedom and confidence to direct your customer or subject expertly. You will have removed one major impediment, allowing you to focus on your delivery, tone, breath, and the freedom to observe your subject. This is quite useful since you will learn a lot by watching how people respond in subtle ways when you speak to them. You can even make changes while the procedure is running. As your abilities improve, you will detect more cues that will allow you to help them go deeper into a trance or make your statements more persuasive.

There are several methods for improving memorisation skills. One approach is to read your manuscript aloud several times. Another option is to videotape yourself saying it and listen to it while walking about or driving in your car. You might also try writing it out numerous times. Association is a technique that can help with memorisation. If you associate what you're saying with another object, it will stick with you. The better you comprehend the method and the meaning of what you're saying, the easier it will be to remember. In your imagination, divide the script into portions. Consider the big strokes as well as the tiny fragments within them. You can constantly reorient yourself in a segment if you become lost. To achieve accuracy and precision, it's best to study these scripts word for word. The more you practise them, the more colour and feel you'll add while working with individuals.

Language and Word Choice

They say that a picture is worth a thousand words. As hypnotists, we need words to create images, and for that, we need imagination and an extensive vocabulary! Many people believe that your vision serves as a bridge between conscious and subconscious minds. This extraordinary phenomenon is unique to humans and opens up many new possibilities. To be an effective hypnotist, you must stimulate your client's or subject's imagination as much as possible. How do you go about doing this?

You accomplish this through the use of language. You want them to envision, see, feel, taste, and touch what you say and propose to immerse themselves in the experience fully.

Imagination is tricky; it involves all of the senses, some of which are more evoked than others. Different people react differently to different senses or prefer one sense over another. Visualising and forming an image of something is a very effective means of bringing it into being. Many successful entrepreneurs, athletes, health care professionals, and world leaders employ visualisation to achieve their objectives. The trick here is to experience it completely. Your role as a hypnotist is to utilise your words to enable the individual you're guiding to have the most complete and rich experience possible. Precision is a necessary component. If someone wants to lose weight, they should be specific and say they want to shed 20 pounds. Declare clearly if they have an athletic aim, such as running for an hour three times each week. If they're going to get married, paint a detailed and colourful picture of the wedding. How much should they earn if they want to make more money? What do you mean? How much work did you expend? How much time is spent on that? What exactly are they grappling with if they have a performance-related goal?

How exactly do you want to be in such a situation?

Here's an example of a script that makes use of as many of your senses as possible to create an immersive experience. After you've finished this one, try your hand at writing your own. Start with your own dreams, or persuade a buddy to participate and create something for them.

This is for someone who wants to move into their ideal home. Below, you'll notice that each sense has been divided. It's a good idea to blend them and experiment with emphasising distinct experiences:

Vision

You enter the apartment through the front door and are greeted by a lovely bright living area. From the floor to the ceiling, glass windows provide a glimpse of the metropolis of London below. To your left, there is a modern fireplace and a cosy rug on the floor—white furniture with pastel outlines. Your dog, a cheerful golden retriever, is sitting by the fire.

Hearing

You can hear soft classical music playing in the background, as well as your husband speaking on the phone in the other room. His voice is deep and low. He greets you with a greeting and tells you he'll be right there.

Smell

As you walk into the kitchen to get a glass of wine before dinner, you smell roast chicken and potatoes cooking in the oven and a faint aroma of salad dressing on the salad.

Taste

You sip the wine, a red merlot, and enjoy the beautiful kitchen in front of you. The stainless steel fridge and stove, as well as the lovely handmade ceramic dishes on the kitchen table. You take a couple of almonds from the countertop bowl. They have a sweet and woody flavor.

CHAPTER 7:

SELF-HYPNOSIS TO ELIMINATE BAD HABITS

Let us start by going through how self-hypnosis works. It is the process of providing strong recommendations to your subconscious mind, which then pushes your conscious mind and physical body to attain your goals. As a result, this strategy has been found to be quite beneficial in treating and overcoming harmful habits, including addictions.

Some unpleasant behaviours are more challenging to eliminate than others. If you can muster the desire to do so, you may be able to eliminate certain undesirable behaviours from your life. However, if you notice that despite your best efforts to summon all of your willpower and rational thought process, you are unable to break any of your negative habits, you must realise that the problem is more severe than you imagined.

Logical reasoning abilities and willpower occur at the conscious mind level. The ingredients that cause long-term behavioural changes are found at the subconscious level, where beliefs, emotions, habits, values, intuition, and the power of your imagination are stored. As a result, if you wish to break a harmful habit, you must first connect with your subconscious mind, which self-hypnosis facilitates.

It is critical to realise that self-hypnosis is not a cure-all. It would be foolish to expect to be entirely cured after just one session of self-hypnosis. No, it does not work that way. Keep in mind that you are both the therapist and the patient with self-hypnosis. Similarly to how a therapist works hard to connect with their patient, you must work hard to communicate with your subconscious to root out harmful habits through powerful self-suggestions.

Self-hypnosis can be used to heal harmful habits and addictions with the following goals in mind:

- Self-suggestions are used to alleviate the agonising effects of withdrawal symptoms.

- To instil a dislike and aversion towards unhealthy habits and undesirable actions such as addictions and drug usage.

- To have meaningful and profound talks with your subconscious mind without your conscious mind's judgmental attitude.

Steps for Using Self-Hypnosis to Break Bad Habits and Behaviors

Before you begin, focus on yourself and rate your stress level on a scale of 1 to 10; 1 represents perfect relaxation and 10 illustrates extreme stress.

Step 1:

Take a seat in a chair that is comfortable for you. Make sure your hands are on your lap, and your feet are firmly planted on the ground.

Breathe slowly and deliberately, inhaling for four counts through your left nostril and expelling for eight counts through your right nostril. Continue doing this until you feel stable, robust, and ready to move on.

Step 2:

Imagine your favourite colour entering your body through your head, going through every nook and cranny of your body, and finally exiting out of your feet into the ground beneath you. This visualisation is a great technique to relieve stress in your body. Consider the flow of your favourite hue rinsing away and removing stress from your body and thoughts.

Step 3:

Close your eyes and count backwards from 10 to 1, telling yourself that you are becoming calmer with each number.

Step 4:

When you are deeply in a hypnotic 'trance,' repeat the affirmation: I am safe, comfortable, and in this state. Then, use this procedure to break a variety of harmful habits. As an example:

- If you want to go to bed on time every day, repeat the affirmation, 'When I go to bed early, I feel healthy, happy, and charged with energy to fulfil my goals.' Visualise yourself going to bed and waking up early, addressing life's obstacles with renewed vigour.

- If you want to keep to a healthy diet plan, say to yourself, 'With this healthy diet plan, I will feel fit and ready to take control of my life.' Visualise yourself eating nutritious meals and avoiding bad foods. Consider accomplishing your weight loss objectives with this method.

- If you wish to quit smoking, 'quit smoking is the best gift I can give myself and my loved ones.' Consider a life in which you do not succumb to smoking. Consider the joy on your loved ones' faces when you attain this smoke-free condition.

Step 5:

As you go through Step 4, remember to focus on your breath and feel the calm and stress-free feeling surrounding your body and mind. Allow your subconscious mind to come to the fore so you can interact with it and make practical suggestions for it.

Even after you leave this self-hypnotic session, you will be able to carry this soothing experience with you throughout the day, even as you feel energised to eliminate negative behaviours from your life.

Step 6:

Count from 1 to 10 as you move forward, gradually coming out of your hypnotic state and becoming aware of your surroundings. When you are totally out of your self-hypnosis session, rate your stress level and compare it to the level when you began the session.

CHAPTER 8:

HOW TO SET SMART GOALS

Before you can accomplish a goal, you must first establish one. Many people have no purpose in life and simply drift along with the flow. They don't accomplish anything because they lack direction in their lives. If you know such a person, you are undoubtedly aware that they have the potential to achieve great things but are not particularly goal-oriented and hence unsuccessful. On the other hand, some people set their objectives so high that they are nearly impossible to achieve.

Because they are constantly failing, these people become unhappy and chronically uncomfortable.

Every aim that is not achieved is a failure. Even when you reach a goal, you have the impression that it took longer than it should have. If you are this type of person, chances are you are unable to rest and are continually driving yourself. In this instance, you may accomplish a lot, but you may never enjoy it. The fact that you did not attain your goals as quickly as you would have liked hinders you from appreciating your achievements. You grow old before your time, and anxiety and tension deplete your energy and stamina. Your disenchantment develops into melancholy and cynicism.

There is one common fault in both examples above: a lack of ability to achieve reasonable goals to guide you through your life. If you are the type who drifts with the flow, you usually set very modestly or no goals at all. Fear of failure frequently drives this. You've discovered that failing makes you miserable and worried and that if you don't set any goals, you can't fail. Regrettably, both scenarios result in defeat.

Aside from creating goals that are either too high or too low, you may wind up setting goals that are so complicated that you have no means of understanding whether or not you have met your objectives. In this situation, because you cannot articulate your goals and recognise when you have reached them, you instantly conclude that you have failed. For example, you may decide that your life aim is to be successful, and you may devote all of your time and efforts to that purpose. When asked to define success, all you can offer is a hazy idea, but you know that when you see it, you will identify it.

There is no such thing as success in the real world. All you can aspire for is a range of relative triumphs rather than the magical object known as success. If you haven't already done so, your task is to set reasonable, realistic goals for yourself. They are the ones that will give you direction in life, as well as a sense of achievement and accomplishment when you attain them.

There are two kinds of goals: long-term goals and short-term goals. Long-term objectives are the essential things you want to accomplish in your life in the long run, but short-term goals are what you need to do in the interim.

To reach your long-term goals, you must first complete various short-term goals that lead to the long-term ones, such as enrolling in college, selecting the correct courses, passing your tests, accumulating a sufficient number of credit hours, obtaining a college degree and finding work.

Rules to Help You Set Effective Long-Term Goals

- Check to see if the objective is a good fit for you. Keep an eye out for goals that are too ambiguous, too lofty, or too low. It may be beneficial to speak with others and learn from their experiences. Seek input from friends or professionals about whether this is a realistic aim for you.

- Make your long-term goals broad rather than detailed. Making them particular is a recipe for failure. When you make them general, though, you can attain them in various ways. It is more practical, for example, to seek to be an excellent contribution to the welfare of your community rather than to be voted the most outstanding citizen.

- Once you've decided on your long-term goal, break it down into the short-term goals you'll need to accomplish to get there.

Determine the course that your short-term goals must take. In most circumstances, there are multiple paths to achieving a long-term plan. It is not necessary to follow in the footsteps of others. You can approach it in whatever way that feels right for you.

• Begin right now. Begin working on the short-term goals in a disciplined manner. Make a reasonable timetable and bear in mind that worthwhile things usually take time. Most people underestimate the amount of time it takes to complete a task. It is critical to be patient, or you will become worried, tense, and frustrated.

Rules to Help You Set Effective Short-Term Goals

• Short-term goals, like long-term goals, should be attainable. You must keep them tiny and inconspicuous so that they will lead to the long-term aim. You should be able to complete them rather quickly.

- They need to be more explicit. You must specify them sufficiently so that you can decide your next move as well as where you are going.

- You should prepare and arrange your approach to reaching these short-term goals to increase your chances of success.

- Don't exaggerate the situation if you fail to meet one of your short-term goals. Just because you failed or made a mistake doesn't mean you'll never reach your ultimate goal. If you fail to achieve a short-term goal, simply take a step back and try again, or look for another route around the issue.

- Celebrate every time you accomplish a short-term goal.

This is referred regarded by psychologists as rewarding or reinforcing yourself for the desired behaviour, and it is pretty successful. You don't have to lavish yourself with gifts. Consider the following scenario: you are studying for a test. Every time you finish a unit, reward yourself with a nut or a piece of candy. It is best to keep the teams small and the rewards regular.

Setting big rewards after extensive amounts of labour is frequently less successful. This fundamental concept can be applied to any endeavour. However, this does not exclude you from rewarding yourself after completing an enormous task. If you finish a semester or a course, reward yourself with a brief vacation, an expensive dinner, or a present. When you organise your life in this manner, you will appreciate yourself and what you are doing.

Once you've determined your long-term and short-term objectives, you can programme them into your subconscious mind by following the principles for administering autosuggestions. After completing this, don't return your attention to your goals.

When you are overly focused on your goals, you will become too future-oriented to be in the present moment — you will always be on a trip with no destination. Looking too far into the future can cause you to be dissatisfied with the present and, as a result, force you to make unfavourable sacrifices in order to accomplish your goals. If you are constantly focused on your plans and ready to enjoy the future, the future may never arrive.

Setting goals involves both strategy and direction. Once you've formulated ideas, you should put them in the back of your mind and begin to focus on the present.

CHAPTER 9:

HYPNOSIS AND NLP

NLP is frequently used in conjunction with hypnosis. This is done to improve the efficiency of the training and process. The primary goal of hypnosis is to maximise concentration. The goal is to remove all distractions and impediments, leaving the person's mind open for control and manipulation.

Hypnosis is utilised to strengthen the mind's retention in NLP, which is frequently viewed as an abstract skill that can take time to acquire. The combination of the two aids in mind training.

When we are hypnotised, our minds get concentrated on a specific feature or notion. The goal of the hypnotiser or trainers is to eliminate distractions and noise until our focus is solely on one item. We focus on a certain point, which makes our senses more responsive. It also increases the mind's activity and openness by making it more receptive to receiving additional messages. When this occurs, NLP training is included. Points are presented and stressed so that they are remembered. Because we will not be distracted and our minds will be relatively empty, it will be easier for the mind to accept and keep this information for an extended period. Also, in this state, the mind perceives all instructions as facts rather than objectives, directing us to accomplish specific jobs far better. Depending on the issue, there are a variety of alternative ways used. Self-hypnosis can be used to practise NLP without the assistance of a trainer. The following are a few methods for hypnotising yourself for NLP purposes.

- Begin by being at ease. Wear loose-fitting clothing and avoid wearing constrictive objects of clothing such as watches, belts, sashes, and so on. Wear loose-fitting, lightweight clothing that allows you to breathe freely.

- Similarly, make sure you're in a comfortable setting. Allow the room to be clean, smell fresh, and make you feel at ease. Remove any and all distractions and clutter from the room. Turn off the TV, turn off your phone, and avoid using electronic devices for 30 to 45 minutes. Ascertain if the temperature of the space is also appropriate for your needs. The temperature in the room should not be excessively hot or too cold.

- Sit in a comfortable chair in a comfortable position and close the door or ask people not to bother you for a bit.

- After you've settled into a comfortable position, consider your aims and ambitions. Speak to yourself in a clear voice and in the present tense. Also, make sure you speak as if it is already happening. Instead of saying, "I want to quit smoking," say, "I've quit smoking, and I'm feeling a lot better about it."

- Relax both your mind and your body. Maintain proper posture and avoid crossing your arms and legs because you will begin to fidget when you feel discomfort. Concentrate on one portion of your body at a time and try to relax it. Relax each part gradually and imagine a soothing location or setting, such as a garden or a valley. This will help to calm your nerves faster. Use a lot of soft and reassuring imagery. Don't be alarmed if you don't feel entirely at ease. This will heighten the distraction. Allow thoughts to enter your head while attempting to relax.

- Once you feel your body is appropriately relaxed, begin by breathing in and out slowly. Make sure you're paying attention to your breathing. Breathe in as if you were inhaling a pleasant aroma, and exhale as if you were removing all the toxins from your lungs. This process of inhaling and exhaling is beneficial and allows you to relax. Continue this method until you feel as though you are floating. You have entered the hypnotic trance when you reach this stage.

- When this happens, keep repeating your objectives. Use encouraging and pleasant language. Avoid using any derogatory words. Instead of saying, "I don't want to fail," say, "I will succeed with tremendous outcomes." Negative comments are retained in the unconscious portions of the mind and might influence your behaviour. It is also challenging to change the unconscious mind. Visualise your thoughts, behaviours, and imagine that what you're saying is actually happening. You'll be able to see yourself in that circumstance right away, and you'll be overjoyed.

•   After a few moments of this, begin removing your imagination. Instead of visualising and fantasising, start thinking. Begin this technique gently; envision yourself in your current situation. The chair you're sitting in, the room you're in, and the clothes you're wearing are all examples of this. Continue to increase this in real-time until you feel as if you have totally escaped your imagination. After then, slowly open your eyes and breathe in and out slowly and evenly as you do so.

•   You can continue this practice twice to three times every day for a total of 30 minutes. This will boost your ability to achieve your goals and maximise your results.

CHAPTER 10:

PRACTICAL APPLICATIONS OF HYPNOSIS

When using hypnosis, a psychologist must first inform the patient of what hypnosis is and is not. When hypnosis is shown on television, the victim usually ends up quacking like a chicken, nude, or assassinating the president.

Despite the fact that stage and TV show hypnotists have tainted the public's perception of hypnosis, an increasing quantity of scientific studies has discovered its usefulness in treating a wide range of diseases such as phobias, pain, and anxiety, and depression

Hypnosis may induce a very calm state of concentrated attention and inner concentration in the patient, and the technique can be modified for various treatments. Patients can also learn how to hypnotise themselves at home to ease anxiety or depression symptoms, improve sleep, or lessen pain.

Hypnosis has been used to alleviate pain for ages. During the Civil War, army doctors would hypnotise injured soldiers before amputating a limb. Guy H. Montgomery, a psychologist, is one of the most prominent researchers. He has done many studies on pain management and hypnotherapy.

People of all ages can benefit from hypnosis. In teens, hypnosis has been shown to be quite beneficial. Teens learn quickly, and hypnosis can provide them with long-term benefits. Let's take a look at some of the top hypnosis applications.

Confidence

Low self-esteem is one of the key underlying reasons for most undesirable behaviours, such as sustaining toxic relationships and overeating. Most of the time, a person's self-esteem suffers as a result of lousy training from an early age. The subconscious mind can hang onto these misconceptions for the rest of one's life and use them to undermine a person without the person even realising it. The person will be able to access these beliefs and causes through hypnosis.

Weight Management

Hypnosis will teach you the skills you need to manage your eating, eat healthy meals, and find the motivation and time to exercise. Typically, weight loss hypnosis is used to determine why you are eating in such an unhealthy manner. It could be emotions that you associate with certain childhood practices or meals. The hypnotist will next work with the client to resolve the underlying feelings, allowing them to stop influencing their eating patterns.

Once the underlying cause is identified, the insights will be used to reinforce motivation and healthy practices.

Relationship Issues

In this regard, hypnosis produces unexpected results. Forgiveness of the past, communication skills, acceptance, and anger control are just a few of the issues that can benefit from hypnosis in a relationship. The couples may be seen together or individually, depending on what is going on in their relationship. Instead of dwelling on the past, they will attempt to imagine the type of relationship the couple desires, as well as the areas that require improvement.

Stress

Many medical authorities and studies believe that the consequences of stress on life in today's culture are nearly epidemic. Stress may wreak emotional and mental devastation, and it is a significant contributor to the majority of physical problems. By demonstrating to the body and mind an easy method to relax, hypnosis can counteract these consequences. Many people will practise self-hypnosis in order to help them treat themselves.

This will have a significant positive impact on their life, job, and family.

Habitual Actions

Habits are learnt habits that occur over time. The conscious mind believes it has everything under control until it tries to avoid a behaviour, such as nail-biting, and finds it has no choice but to do it. The therapist can connect directly with your subconscious mind while you are hypnotised in order to change these behaviours. That voice inside your head that is continuously saying, "do it, just a little won't hurt", may calm down and may begin to say the opposite. In instances like this, the Energy Awareness Process is commonly applied.

As a patient continues to be hypnotised, the conscious mind's motivation is conveyed to the subconscious, and the patient has the ability to change their behavior.

The following are some of the most prevalent habits that people modify using hypnosis:

- Use of pornography
- Gambling
- Picking your nose
- Nail-biting Teeth
- Grinding

Pain

When it comes to pain, hypnosis can be utilised to treat a variety of conditions. Chronic pain is one of the most prevalent complaints. Hypnosis for chronic pain should not be used as a replacement for medical therapy and is not a cure-all. However, when it comes to chronic pain, the subconscious mind will frequently create conditions for the pain to be felt in bodily parts. Even if the wounds have healed, the reason will continue to associate pain with specific situations and emotions. It is frequently challenging to determine if the pain is produced by real pain or by a subconscious association. Hypnosis can help you go to the root of the problem and assist your body and mind recover together.

Hypnosis can also be utilised before and after surgery. Hypnosis can assist patients in relaxing before surgery by lowering their concerns, allowing them to enter the procedure with a healing and happy mindset. Following surgery, hypnosis can help the patient locate visualisations in their subconscious that they can utilise on their own to speed up their recuperation.

Enhancement of Performance

What if you could be in the zone whenever you wanted instead of waiting for it to happen? Hypnosis teaches people how to get into that zone by employing centring, relaxation, and visualisation techniques. Whether you're taking a test, presenting a project proposal, or hitting a golf ball, hypnosis can help.

Dreamwork

Randall Churchill invented the dreamwork process. It's a method of utilising significant dreams brought to the session by the client. There is no dream interpretation since it can become highly misleading and sophisticated. Instead, they will usually find a solution by using hypnosis and Gestalt Therapy to get an understanding. The most crucial reason for dreamwork is because each part of a dream represents a different aspect of the client.

As a result, conflict in a plan frequently corresponds to competition in the person. Gestalt discourse is commonly utilised as a form of integration during hypnosis.

Regression

Regression is frequently used to determine the root cause of a problem. During a regression session, the client will be transported back to their childhood or older experiences in order to assess the reasons for specific actions or perspectives. During hypnosis, the subconscious is urged to recall memories related to particular situations. The subconscious will then select the appropriate memory associated with the habit or feeling. Any memory that comes to mind must be fair and safe, and you and your subconscious will choose it.

It's natural for many people to be apprehensive about revisiting a former memory, and that's understandable. Everyone has experienced adversity. However, this purpose is to let go of patterns that you are still harboring.

Previous Existence

To get answers, past life regression might be used. It can even benefit those who are dubious of former incarnations. Some people regard past incarnations as a symbolic storey in which the subconscious provides insight into things that cannot be stated differently. Whatever you believe, a past life regression can help you look at your decisions and life in a new light.

People opt to undergo a former life regression because they are curious or because they have heard others talk about it. Others may be drawn to it to assist them in resolving issues they may be having. Some people, however, are concerned that they would be unable to link their symptoms back to a specific event in their past.

Quitting Smoking

Often, hypnosis was used to help people quit smoking by making a recommendation while they were hypnotised. According to a new study, smoking should be treated in the same way as any other habit. You must identify and resolve the root cause of smoking.

The client is given the opportunity to locate that trigger through hypnosis. This method of treatment is successful and aids in long-term abstinence, but it is not a quick fix. The client must be willing to look for the underlying issues that are causing their smoking.

CONCLUSION

Since humans began to research the brain and its functions, hypnosis has been a popular aspect of popular culture. The phrase is derived from the Greek word "Hypnos," which means "sleep." However, the literal translation has become a misnomer as hypnosis has changed and evolved along with its connotation. Hypnosis has become an intriguing and hotly discussed issue due to its charisma, suggestion, and therapy to generate a uniquely human condition known as trance.

Although modern hypnosis was initially brought to the field of medicine in the late 18th century, the concept of hypnosis as we know it now first reached the public eye in the late 1930s. As you can see, hypnosis has been relevant and present in the world for a very long time—it is neither a fad nor a passing craze. No, hypnosis isn't as mystical as some may portray it to be. Hypnosis is a highly scientific technique that aids in the relief of pain, the treatment of mental illnesses, and the reduction of general suffering in the lives of many individuals.

Hypnosis has progressed from a secret technique to a stage show, a party trick—of course, it's also being utilised more successfully in therapy than ever before. This rise of hypnosis and its media attraction invites the question, "Why is it so fascinating?" What is it about hypnosis that makes it so appealing?

The solution is most likely found in our fascination with sleep and the afterlife. Although hypnosis has a tenuous connection to what happens after we die, it nonetheless represents the unknown. Because hypnosis, despite its age, is still a relatively young area of research in the world of medicine, we have yet to comprehend it fully. Every day, many hypnosis scientists and researchers propose new hypotheses on hypnosis, hypnotic trance, induction, suggestion, and a variety of other topics. We look for more mystical explanations for the process since we know so little about it. In the same way, as the afterlife does, we fill in blanks with imaginative notions and possibilities.

Hypnosis evolved from a mysterious therapeutic area to a sort of overdone party trick somewhere along the road. Although it is frequently overstated, this party trick has the same efficacy as therapeutic hypnosis.

Although television and the media have presented this type of hypnosis as sinister or ridiculous, recreational hypnosis has a sizable following, and that recreational hypnosis, with placebo, fills in the gaps of actual experience or a medical degree. The charisma and confidence of a hypnotist are what ultimately promotes hypnosis as a therapeutic or recreational technique; thus, individuals entranced in the hypnotist's "show" pay less attention to any technical errors that may have occurred. This is also why those who are prone to daydreaming and have difficulty focusing are more susceptible to hypnosis and trance.

Because humans have a bizarre obsession with loss of control, hypnosis may be considered a fascinating issue to society today. Although hypnosis isn't strictly a complete loss of control, we do cease to be completely autonomous and independent while under trance, so it's possible that we're fascinated by that sensation. We are frequently afflicted by stress in our lives, and techniques to reduce that tension are aggressively advertised in the same way that water, soda, and candy are. Hypnosis is a compelling approach to relieve stress momentarily—you can't be stressed about something if you've stopped thinking things the way you're used to.

We remove most/all sources of stress from the hypnotic subject for the duration of the session if we turn off the conscious mind and feed the subconscious only good information. Furthermore, many recreational and therapeutic hypnotists like to include post-hypnotic recommendations that leave the client feeling relaxed, focused, and joyful even after the session is over. Depending on the proposal and the subject, these suggestions can last for any period. Some recommendations can be made in minutes, while others might be made in weeks.

Those suggestions may have to be eliminated by the same hypnotist who implanted them in the subject. However, if the issue is aware of it and strongly opposes the suggestion, most individuals may erase it or allow it to fade into the background of the subconscious mind.

That subconscious mind is crucial in developing the relationship that inevitably develops and grows between a hypnotic subject and their hypnotist. When the subconscious is exposed in this manner, even if the exchange isn't intended to be romantic, the experience itself is designed to be a very intimate interaction between the two people. Hypnosis is frequently a repeated encounter involving the same pair of persons, the same subject, and the hypnotist working together.

Because these two persons work with one other so frequently, the hypnotist and subject often become very devoted to one another. As a hypnotist, it might be difficult to avoid making a connection with your issue. Even as novice or beginner hypnotists, all people have a mild need to care for those around us. When we put a subject in a trance and observe the pure and raw trust that the issue has placed in their hypnotist, we can't help but try our hardest to fulfil that trust and provide a satisfactory experience for the subject. That trust is a hidden function of hypnosis—the development of a connection takes a back seat to the appeal of persuasion and control, but that relationship should never be overlooked by either participant.

To be sure, hypnosis is not as extensively employed as the public's obsession with any method of stress relief would suggest. However, this could simply be because many people do not believe hypnosis is natural in the first place. It could also be due to the fact that many therapists are not certified in hypnosis. However, stress alleviation through hypnosis does not have to be sought simply through therapeutic procedures.

Most of the same components are present in recreational hypnosis; however, the purpose of recreational hypnosis is to focus on the subject's pleasure/fun rather than assisting them with a significant mental problem or trauma they may have suppressed. It's possible that when the hypnotist or partner is someone you trust more than a therapist you don't know, the subject has a much easier time relaxing and enjoying the session.

Of course, some folks are simply too stressed out to enter trance correctly. Those who suffer from persistent worry or stress to a great degree are likely to have considerably more difficulty relaxing and focusing on one subject, necessitating the assistance of a veteran or experienced hypnotherapist. There is no one who cannot be hypnotised, but living in a condition of panic for the majority of your life does not help your case. If this is your first hypnosis session, keep in mind that the capacity to relax and focus is what makes hypnosis work most of the time. These two factors are essential for a successful and happy trance. Taking deep breaths and keeping your pulse rate low are effective first measures to preparing yourself to be hypnotised, especially since a hypnotist's first request is usually to begin breathing deeply and gently.

Counting 3 seconds of inhalation and 5 seconds of exhalation may help, but different things work for other people.

However, the power of hypnosis is derived from your and my minds. The power of believing in hypnosis is what causes it to work in the first place. Of course, if you don't believe in it, it goes away. If you believe in it, hypnosis is as natural as any otherworldly or mental force. When viewed in this light, "thought over matter" demonstrates its validity.